Be Your Own Shaman:

Science, Mysticism and Psilocybin

333 Publishing

New York, New York

ISBN: 978-1-951231-11-8

Table of Contents

Introduction

A psilocybin mushroom is one of a polyphyletic group of fungi that contain any of various psychedelic compounds, including psilocybin, psilocin, and baeocystin. Biological genera containing psilocybin mushrooms include Copelandia, Gymnopilus, Inocybe, Mycena, Panaeolus, Pholiotina, Pluteus, and Psilocybe. Present in varying concentrations in about two hundred species of Basidiomycota mushrooms, psilocybin evolved from its ancestor, muscarine, some ten to twenty million years ago. In a 2000 review on the worldwide distribution of psilocybin mushrooms, Gastón Guzmán and colleagues considered these distributed among the following genera: Psilocybe (116 species), Gymnopilus (14), Panaeolus (13), Copelandia (12), Hypholoma (6), Pluteus (6) Inocybe (6), Conocybe (4), Panaeolina (4), Gerronema (2), Agrocybe (1), Galerina (1) and Mycena (1). Guzmán increased his estimate of the number of psilocybin-containing Psilocybe to 144 species in a 2005 review. Many of these are found in Mexico (53 species), with the remainder distributed in Canada and the US (22), Europe (16), Asia (15), Africa (4), and Australia and associated islands (19). At present, psilocybin mushroom use has been reported among some groups spanning from central Mexico to Oaxaca, including groups of Nahua, Mixtecs, Mixe, Mazatecs, Zapotecs, and others. In general, psilocybin-containing species are dark-spored, gilled mushrooms that grow in meadows and woods of the subtropics and tropics, usually in soils rich in humus and plant debris. Psilocybin mushrooms occur on all continents, but the majority of species are found in subtropical humid forests. Psilocybe species commonly found in the tropics include P. cubensis and P. subcubensis. P. semilanceata, considered the world's most widely distributed psilocybin mushroom, is found in Europe, North America, Asia, South America, Australia and New Zealand, although it is absent from Mexico. Common, colloquial terms for psilocybin mushrooms include psychedelic mushrooms, booms, magic mushrooms, shrooms, and mush. An important figure of mushroom usage in Mexico was María Sabina, who used native mushrooms, such as Psilocybe Mexicana, in her practice, which attracted the likes of Bob Dylan, John Lennon, the Rolling Stones and Pele.

Alexander Shulgin wrote in his classic, *A Chemical Love Story*, that "I am completely convinced that there is a wealth of information built into us, with miles of intuitive knowledge tucked away in the genetic material of every one of our cells. Something akin to a library containing uncountable reference volumes, but without any obvious route of entry. And, without some means of access, there is no way to even begin to guess at the extent and quality of what is there. The psychedelic drugs allow exploration of this interior world, and insights into its nature."

Indeed. The thesis of this text is thus very simple: religious and scientific research support the revolutionary idea that psilocybin has, can, and should be considered to be a very good thing for human beings, both individually as well as for any society that professes to sanctify Enlightenment Era notions such as liberty, fraternity, and equality. The pages that follow do not contain stories of "psychedelic experiences" from "psychonauts." This publication is broken into two interrelated sections that focus on psilocybin in the context of enduring humanistic concepts, namely science and religion. One of the goals of this text is to erode the duality, this false consciousness, between science and religion.

Part one considers psilocybin in the realm of science. It is broken into four small chapters. Chapter one provides a short history of psilocybin as used in scientific research since the nineteenth century. Chapter two provides a concise neurological explanation of what scientists believe happens to the human brain and body when under the influence of psilocybin. Chapter three provides an explication of, based on research to date, the personal benefits of taking psilocybin. The fourth and final chapter in part one of the text provides a concise explication of the apparent societal benefits of taking psilocybin.

Part two of the text delves into psilocybin in the realm of metaphysics, which includes a short history of the psilocybin containing mushroom as a sacrament used in ancient religious ceremonies. The second chapter in part two provides an examination of psilocybin as having aided in mystical and religious experiences amongst many who ingested it. These "mystical experiences" can be rather accurately qualified and quantified. The third chapter in part two delves into the legal status of psilocybin around the world, and provides some useful legal precedents that might help one craft a legal defense rooted in freedom of religion supposedly protected by the first amendment to the United States Constitution; a clause that might be of particular importance to anyone wishing to cultivate her own psilocybin for sacramental use. The text concludes with an extensive chapter that includes a step-by-step guide on producing your own psilocybin for sacramental use. These directions are followed by guidelines for usage.

Chapter One

"A Concise History of Psychedelics in the Laboratory"

The first mention of hallucinogenic mushrooms in European medicinal literature appeared in the *London Medical and Physical Journal* in 1799: a man had served Psilocybe semilanceata mushrooms that he had picked for breakfast in London's Green Park to his family. The doctor who treated them later described how the youngest child was "attacked with fits of immoderate laughter, nor could the threats of his father or mother refrain him." It was another century before psychedelic drug research began in earnest; in 1897 German chemist Arthur Heffter first isolated mescaline, the primary psychoactive compound in the peyote cactus. William James' *The Varieties of Religious Experience,* published five years later in 1902, did much to illuminate the effectiveness of psychedelics such as psilocybin in inducing mystical experiences in those who consumed them.

But it was not until the twentieth century that mainstream scientists in the United States and Europe began to take an earnest interest in psychedelic drug effects. A Swiss scientist named Albert Hoffman first created LSD in a laboratory in an attempt to duplicate natural psychedelic substances. By the 1950s, LSD became a commonly used psychiatric treatment for a variety of conditions, some of which include alcoholism, schizophrenia and other personality disorders. Throughout the 1950s and 1960s, psychedelics were used in clinical studies within various psychotherapeutic approaches.

In 1955, Valentina Pavlovna Wasson and R. Gordon Wasson became the first known European Americans to actively participate in an indigenous mushroom ceremony. The Wassons did much to publicize their discovery, even publishing an article on their experiences in *Life* in 1957. In 1956, Roger Heim identified the psychoactive mushroom that the Wassons had brought back from Mexico as Psilocybe, and in 1958, Albert Hofmann first identified psilocybin and psilocin as the active compounds in these mushrooms.

Inspired by the Wassons' *Life* article, Timothy Leary traveled to Mexico to experience psilocybin mushrooms firsthand. Upon returning to Harvard in 1960, he and Richard Alpert started the Harvard Psilocybin Project, promoting psychological and religious study of psilocybin and other psychedelic drugs. After Leary and Alpert were dismissed by Harvard in 1963, they turned their attention toward promoting the psychedelic experience to the nascent hippie counterculture. In 1964, Leary, Alpert, and Ralph Metzner published *The Psychedelic Experience: A Manual Based on the Tibetan Book of the Dead*.

The popularization of entheogens by Wasson, Leary, authors Terence McKenna and Robert Anton Wilson, and others led to an explosion in the use of psilocybin mushrooms throughout the world. By the early 1970s, many psilocybin mushroom species were described from temperate North America, Europe, and Asia and were widely collected. Books describing methods of cultivating Psilocybe cubensis in large quantities were also published. The availability of psilocybin mushrooms from wild and cultivated sources has made it among the most widely used of the psychedelic drugs.

Already by the mid-1960s, psychedelics saw widespread use within the hippie counterculture, with LSD becoming the most popular of all. Within the history of psychedelics, LSD use became a symbol of youthful rebellion, mind exploration and political dissent on college campuses across the United States. This widespread use of LSD soon caught the attention of federal and state governments, so much so that it was made an illegal substance in 1967. Richard Nixon famously referred to Leary as "the most dangerous man in America."

Within the U.S., the early 1970s saw an across-the-board ban on any scientific research involving psychedelic drugs. Possession and use of these drugs also became illegal. In the 1990s, ecstasy replaced LSD as the new "party" drug. During this time, government regulations also lifted bans on research studies that examined the medical safety and possible uses for psychedelics as medical treatments. This long history of psychedelic use for religious and medicinal purposes has, however, ultimately paved the way for further investigation on the actual benefits of psychedelic drugs.

Before 1972 close to 700 studies with psychedelic drugs took place. The research suggested that psychedelics offered significant benefits: they helped recovering alcoholics abstain, soothed the anxieties of terminal cancer patients, and eased the symptoms of many difficult-to-treat psychiatric illnesses, such as obsessive-compulsive disorder. For example, between 1967 and 1972 studies in terminal cancer patients by psychiatrist Stanislav Grof and his colleagues at Spring Grove State Hospital in Baltimore showed that LSD combined with psychotherapy could alleviate symptoms of depression, tension, anxiety, sleep disturbances, psychological withdrawal and even severe physical pain. Other investigators during this era found that LSD may have some interesting potential as a means to facilitate creative problem solving.

But between 1972 and 1990 there were no human studies with psychedelic drugs. Their disappearance was the result of a political backlash that followed the promotion of these drugs by the 1960s counterculture. This reaction not only made these substances illegal for personal use but also made it extremely difficult for researchers to get government approval to study them. Many groups, however, formed to challenge the federal government's death sentence of publicly funded psychedelic research. Founded in 1986, the Multidisciplinary Association for Psychedelic Studies (MAPS), is a 501(c)(3) non-profit research and educational organization that develops medical, legal, and cultural contexts for people to benefit from the careful uses of psychedelics and marijuana. The Heffter Research Institute formed in 1993. Outside the U.S. there are groups such as the Beckley Foundation in England and the Russian Psychedelic Society. These seek out interested researchers, assist in developing the experimental design for the studies, and help to obtain funding and government approval to conduct clinical trials. They have initiated numerous FDA approved clinical trials in the U.S., Switzerland, Israel and Spain.

So far the agency has approved seven studies, with two under review and more on the way. Current studies focus on psychedelic treatments for cluster headaches, depression, obsessive-compulsive disorder (OCD), severe anxiety in terminal cancer patients, post-traumatic stress disorder (PTSD), alcoholism and opiate addiction.

New drugs must pass three clinical milestones before they can be marketed to the public, called phase I (for safety, usually in 20 to 80 volunteers), phase II (for efficacy, in several hundred subjects) and phase III (more extensive data on safety and efficacy come from testing the drug in up to several thousand people). All the studies discussed in this article have received government approval, and their investigators are either in the process of recruiting human subjects or have begun or completed research on human subjects in the first or second stage of this trial process.

"Psychedelics may be therapeutic to the extent that they elicit processes that are known to be useful in a therapeutic context: transference reactions and working through them; enhanced symbolism and imagery; increased suggestibility; increased contact between emotions and ideations; controlled regression; et cetera," says psychiatrist Rick Strassman of the University of New Mexico School of Medicine, who from 1990 to 1995 performed the first human study using psychedelic drugs in about 20 years, investigating the effects of DMT on sixty human subjects. "This all depends, though, on set and setting," he cautions. "These same properties could also be turned to very negative experiences, if the support and expectation for a beneficial experience aren't there."

In 2006, investigators at the Johns Hopkins School of Medicine published the results of a six-year project on the effects of psilocybin, in which more than sixty percent of the participants reported positive changes in their attitude and behavior after taking the drug, a benefit that lasted for at least several months. In another 2006 study, researchers at the University of Arizona, led by psychiatrist Francisco Moreno, found that psilocybin relieved the symptoms of nine patients with OCD. The patients suffered from a wide range of obsessions and compulsions. Some of them showered for hours; others put on their clothes over and over again until they felt right. All nine experienced improvements with at least some of the doses tested. "What we saw was a drastic decrease in symptoms for a period of time," Moreno says. "People would report that it had been years since they had felt so good." Moreno, however, cautions that the goal was simply to test the safety of administering psilocybin to OCD patients and that the true effectiveness of the drug is still in question until a larger controlled study can be conducted. Such a study is being planned, although there were when Brown's article was published in 2008, no funds available for it. According to Moreno, however, no treatment in the medical literature eases OCD symptoms as fast as psilocybin does. Whereas other drugs take several weeks to show an effect, psilocybin worked almost immediately.

Preliminary results of a current study led by psychiatrist Charles Grob of the Harbor-UCLA Medical Center suggest that psilocybin may reduce the psychological distress associated with terminal cancer. This research seeks to measure the effectiveness of psilocybin on the reduction of anxiety, depression and physical pain in advanced-stage cancer patients. "My impression," Grob said, "from just staying in touch with these people and following them is that some do seem to be functioning better psychologically. There seems to be less anxiety, improved mood and an overall improved quality of life. There also seemed to be less fear of death."[1]

Johns Hopkins psychopharmacologist Roland R. Griffiths and his colleagues found in their study that psilocybin frequently sparked temporary mystical makeovers in volunteers who didn't know

---

[1] David Jay Brown, "Psychedelic Healing?" *Scientific American Mind*, Vol. 18, No. 6 (December 2007/January 2008), pp. 66-71.

what kind of pill they were taking. What's more, some of these participants reported long-lasting positive effects of their experiences.

Methylphenidates such as MDMA, conversely, rarely produced a mystical experience. "With careful preparation," Griffiths explained, "you can safely and fairly reliably occasion a mystical experience using psilocybin that may lead to positive changes in a person... Our finding is an early step in what we hope will be scientific work that helps people."

Griffiths' recent work was inspired by an unusual 1963 investigation conducted by physician and minister Walter Pahnke. Pahnke, a theology graduate student at the Harvard Divinity School who had already earned a medical degree (M.D.), devised the Marsh Chapel Experiment as the basis for his dissertation. He was curious to trace empirically if, in religiously predisposed subjects, psilocybin would act as a reliable entheogen. To Pahnke's amazement, half of twenty Protestant seminarians randomly received psilocybin before listening to a radio broadcast of a Good Friday service. The rest took a B-vitamin. After the service, many members of the psilocybin group reported unusual spiritual experiences. Four of them had full-blown mystical reactions, which they said included ecstatic visions and a feeling of oneness with God. In interviews conducted six months and twenty-five years later, members of the psilocybin group attributed many more positive changes in attitude and behavior to the Good Friday service than vitamin takers did. Psilocybin-induced mental states had apparently triggered lasting improvements in people's lives, researchers concluded. "There's good reason to believe that similar brain mechanisms are at work during profound religious experiences, whether they're produced by fasting, meditation, controlled breathing, sleep deprivation, near death experiences, infectious disease states, or psychoactive substances," Griffiths says.[2]

There are also studies underway at Johns Hopkins and NYU where they're treating terminal

---

[2] Bruce Bower "Chemical Enlightenment," *Science News*, Vol. 170, No. 14 (Sep. 30, 2006), pp. 216-217+220.

cancer patients for what they call "existential distress." These are people who are facing their own death with a blend of anxiety and depression and fear that people with a cancer diagnosis often feel. There's a researcher at the University of California at Berkeley named Dacher Keltner who studies awe, and he suggests that it shrinks the ego, that it results in something he calls the "small self." You're in the presence of something so large that your own sense of self is dwarfed by it. That's a very positive and socially useful emotion. You can reconnect to others after an experience of awe. So that's one explanation for why psychedelics such as psilocybin have been so successful in treating such a wide array of issues. Matt Johnson, one of the researchers at Johns Hopkins, says that we have these stories we tell ourselves about ourselves, and we get stuck on them. We tell ourselves that we're not worthy of love, that we can't get through the next hour without a cigarette, and Johnson thinks these psychedelic experiences shake us out of these patterns because suddenly we see them from a new perspective.

Philosopher Chris Letheby believes that psychedelic drugs are a legitimate way to achieve a spiritual and therapeutic transformation. His doctoral research at the University of Adelaide was the first systematic attempt to relate psychedelic experience and twenty-first century philosophy of cognitive science. He argued in his thesis that psychedelics can be rightfully regarded as bringing a deeper understanding of ourselves and the world around us. In fact, he says, the use of psychedelics is very much consistent with philosophical naturalism and our current scientific knowledge. While using psychedelics, Letheby maintains, subjects gain knowledge of their own psychological potential and the fact that their selves are constructed. Letheby argues that as recent scientific evidence shows, psychedelic sessions can lead to the reduction in the symptoms of anxiety, addiction and depression. Since these activities prevent people from engaging with the world, our normal way of gaining knowledge, psychedelics provide what Letheby calls "epistemic benefits" - allowing the patients to get reconnected

and be able to once again take in information. He
described his philosophy as "physicalism or
materialism" that basically says the mind and
consciousness emerge from "the complex
organization of non-minded, non-conscious things."
He thinks that from that standpoint, psychedelic
states can allow the subjects to gain "genuine
knowledge" of psychology.

Although still in the early days of psychedelic
therapy research, the initial data show considerable
promise. A growing number of scientists believe that
psychedelic drugs may offer safe and effective help
for people with certain treatment-resistant psychiatric
disorders and could possibly help some people who
receive partial relief from current methods to obtain a
more complete healing. The psychedelic revolution, at
least in the realm of medical research, might not be
too far beyond the horizon. In recent years
psychedelic research has slowly returned to the
mainstream — with university scientists and
nonprofits like the Multidisciplinary Association for
Psychedelic Studies introducing a sober, FDA-

approved, clinical approach. In the process science and religion have a greater recognition of how psychedelics can form new connections in the brain and introduce new perspectives, helping patients overcome addiction, anxiety, depression, and PTSD.

Chapter Two

"Physiological Effects of Psilocybin on Humans"

In 2017, *VICE's* Susan Rinkunas published an article titled, "Psychedelic Drugs Really Do Lead to a Higher State of Consciousness." She noted that scientists had found the first evidence of a higher state of consciousness and, unsurprisingly, it was in the brains of people who were tripping. For the study, published in the *Journal Scientific Reports*, researchers at the University of Sussex reanalyzed brain scans of healthy volunteers who took one of three psychedelic drugs: ketamine, LSD, or psilocybin, or a placebo. (A team from Imperial College London and the University of Cardiff collected the initial data.) The scans looked for tiny magnetic fields produced in subjects' brains to measure neural signal diversity, or the complexity of brain activity.

The diversity of brain signals is a mathematical index for the level of consciousness; people who are awake have more diverse brain signal activity than people who are asleep, under anesthesia, or in a vegetative state, for example. The researchers found that all three drugs produced higher levels of brain signal diversity than the baseline "awake" state observed in people in the placebo group. They found similar changes in signal diversity even though the drugs are very different, pharmacologically, and noted that people who reported more intense experiences had more brain signal changes. This doesn't necessarily mean that people who got the drugs were thinking more philosophically, or that this is a "better" brain state; just that their brains operated at a different, higher level than normal. "During the psychedelic state, the electrical activity of the brain is less predictable and less 'integrated' than during normal conscious wakefulness — as measured by 'global signal diversity,'" Anil Seth, co-director of the Sackler Centre for Consciousness Science at the University of Sussex, said in a release. "Since this measure has already shown its value as a measure of 'conscious level,' we can say that the psychedelic state appears as a higher 'level' of consciousness than normal — but only with respect to this specific mathematical measure."

Robin Cahart-Harris, head of psychedelic research at Imperial College London, one of the schools that conducted the original experiment, said that "the present study's findings help us understand what happens in people's brains when they experience an expansion of their consciousness under psychedelics. People often say they experience insight under these drugs — and when this occurs in a therapeutic context, it can predict positive outcomes. The present findings may help us understand how this can happen."

One of the things that is established in neuroscience is the existence of the Default Mode Network. This is, evolutionarily speaking, the most recent part of the brain to develop, and it is closely connected to the brain regions responsible for memories and emotions. This network thus seems to play some kind of regulatory role in how the brain communicates with itself. One neuroscientist referred to it as the orchestra conductor of the neural symphony. Based on fMRI imaging, some neuroscientists think DMN is involved in our ability to imagine the mental states of someone else and in our own self-reflection. When humans think about ourselves, when we worry about the past or feel anxious about the future, this is our DMN at work. The DMN also helps us create a consistent story of ourselves across time, which is key to the formation of self-identity. The DMN is also how humans take in new information and link it up to stories we tell ourselves about who we have been and who we want to be. The ability to slow the DMN is why psychedelics might be so important to treating depression and mental health problems. When you look at the brains of people who are on psilocybin or LSD or other psychedelics, you find that the DMN goes quiet; it doesn't shut down completely, but it's significantly diminished. And when this happens, people experience a temporary death of the ego. This is important because as the brain imagery shows, the brain starts to form new linkages and new connections. Parts of the brain that did not previously communicate before suddenly strike up conversations. Scientists are not close to fully understanding this yet, but they believe this is when new insights and new perspectives are formed in the brain, and this can be a tremendously powerful experience.

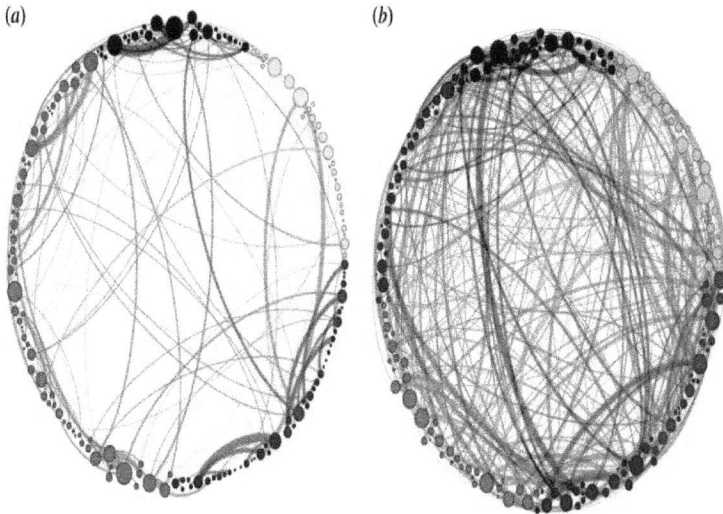

This figure is from a 2014 study in the *Journal of the Royal Society Interface*. The image on the left is of a human brain on a placebo, and the image on the right is of a brain on psilocybin.

When Timothy Leary advised his generation to "turn on" by taking psychedelic drugs, he, in short, actually got it wrong. Turning off parts of the brain may be the real secret to expanding your mind, research reported by the National Academy of Sciences concludes. "The findings are astounding and are going to completely change how we understand the action of hallucinogens," says psychiatrist and pharmacologist Bryan Roth of the University of North Carolina at Chapel Hill. The study discovered that the hubs that connect different parts of the brain, including the thalamus and parts of the cingulate cortex actually slow down when under the influence of psilocybin. "Decreasing the activity in certain hubs in the network may allow for a more unconstrained conscious experience," says Matthew Johnson, an experimental psychologist at Johns Hopkins University School of Medicine who studies psilocybin and other hallucinogens. "These drugs may lift the filters that are at play in terms of limiting our perception of reality."[3]

Scientists divide classical psychedelic drugs into two basic chemical groups: tryptamines (such as LSD, DMT and psilocybin) and phenethylamines (such as mescaline and MDMA). The exact mechanisms differ, but all the tryptamine

---

[3] Devin Powell, "Psychedelics chill brain out," *Science News*, Vol. 181, No. 4 February 25, 2012), p. 8.

hallucinogens — which make up the majority of
psychedelic drugs — selectively bind to specific
serotonin receptors on neurons, mimicking the effects
of the nerve-signaling chemical, or neurotransmitter,
serotonin on these receptors. Phenethylamines mimic
the chemical structure of another neurotransmitter,
dopamine. They actually bind to many of the same
serotonin receptors activated by the tryptamines,
however. Serotonin is responsible for many important
functions, including mood, memory, appetite, sex and
sleep. It is such an essential neurochemical that any
substance — such as a hallucinogen — that interferes
with its action might be expected to produce dramatic
changes in brain function. How do the drugs create
their perceptual effects? Neuroscientists believe that
activation of a particular set of serotonin receptors,
the 2A subtype, which are highly expressed (or
present) in the cortex, the outermost layer of the
brain, interferes with the processing of sensory
information. Consciousness is thought to involve a
complex interaction among the cortex, the thalamus
and the striatum. Disruption of this network by

activation of serotonin 2A receptors is now the most popular theory for the mechanism of action for tryptamine and phenethylamine psychedelics. [4]

Psychedelic drugs affect all mental functions: perception, emotion, cognition, body awareness and one's sense of self. The effects of psilocybin mushrooms come from psilocybin and psilocin. When psilocybin is ingested, it is broken down to produce psilocin, which is responsible for the psychedelic effects. Psilocybin and psilocin create short-term increases in tolerance of users, thus making it difficult to abuse them because the more often they are taken within a short period of time, the weaker the resultant effects are. Psilocybin mushrooms have also not been known to cause physical or psychological dependence (addiction).

As with many psychedelic substances, the effects of psychedelic mushrooms are subjective and can vary considerably among individual users. The

---

[4] David Jay Brown, "Psychedelic Healing?" *Scientific American Mind*, Vol. 18, No. 6 (December 2007/January 2008), pp. 66-71.

mind-altering effects of psilocybin containing mushrooms typically last from three to eight hours depending on dosage, preparation method, and personal metabolism. The first three to four hours of the trip are typically referred to as the 'peak' — in which the user experiences more vivid visuals, and distortions in reality. However, the effects can seem to last much longer to the user because of psilocybin's ability to alter time perception.

Sensory effects include visual and auditory hallucinations followed by emotional changes and altered perception of time and space. Noticeable changes to the auditory, visual, and tactile senses may become apparent around thirty minutes to an hour after ingestion, although effects may take up to two hours to take place. These shifts in perception visually include enhancement and contrasting of colors, strange light phenomena (such as auras or "halos" around light sources), increased visual acuity, surfaces that seem to ripple, shimmer, or breathe; complex open and closed eye visuals of form constants or images, objects that warp, morph, or change solid colors; a sense of melting into the environment, and trails behind moving objects. Sounds may seem to have increased clarity — music, for example, can take on a profound sense of cadence and depth. Some users experience synesthesia, wherein they perceive, for example, a visualization of color upon hearing a particular sound. As with other psychedelics such as LSD, the experience, or 'trip,' is strongly dependent upon set and setting. A negative environment could contribute to a bad trip, whereas a comfortable and familiar environment would set the stage for a pleasant experience. Psychedelics make experiences more intense, so if a person enters a trip in an anxious state of mind, they will likely experience heightened anxiety on their trip. Many users find it preferable to ingest the mushrooms with friends or people who are familiar with 'tripping.'

Chapter Three

"Psilocybin and Personal Well-Being"

"For far too long, mental health treatment has rested heavily on SSRI antidepressants. Patients need to take these every day; they have no beneficial effect for at least thirty percent of users, with numerous side effects," says Amanda Feilding, director of the Beckley Foundation, a United Kingdom-based think tank at the forefront of psychedelic research and drug policy reform. "Furthermore, the pharmaceutical industry hasn't come up with anything new for over three decades. Our research has shown that with the addition of a psychedelic to the therapeutic process we get remarkable results." For years, the field of mental health has been largely barren of meaningful treatment advances. But now, scientists have new hope – psychedelic drugs. Recent research suggests that certain psychedelic substances, including psilocybin, can help relieve anxiety, depression, PTSD, addiction and the fear surrounding a terminal diagnosis. "Psychedelics alter the mind in such a way that they reveal aspects of the mind that we are not ordinarily conscious about. In the last seventy years, psychiatry has been dominated by the cognitive model of the mind, which has brought interesting insights, but has also impoverished the field by denying the existence of the unconscious mind," says Robin Carhart-Harris, a neuroscientist at Imperial College London who has worked extensively with psychedelics. "We need an understanding of the unconscious mind, otherwise we'll only ever have a superficial knowledge of psychiatric diseases, and superficial treatments."

Psilocybin and many other psychedelics are classified under Schedule I of the Controlled Substances Act, meaning they're considered to have a high potential for abuse and are of no current medical value. Despite that designation (and the legal hurdles around working with Schedule I drugs), psychedelics have undergone something of a renaissance among researchers. Even use outside of a medical setting has shown an association with decreased psychological distress, domestic violence, psychoses, and suicidality. Psilocybin has been tried as an antidepressant, with particular success treating anxiety and depression among cancer patients. It's also been used to treat addiction. Meanwhile, outside the lab, there's the emergence of micro-dosing: taking small, regular doses of psychedelics to boost creativity and, of course, productivity. All of which suggests that maybe this broad class of substances has some medical value. Researchers wanted to see if, given the apparent success in treating addiction, psychedelics might be useful in combating the opioid epidemic. Using data from the National Survey on Drug Use and Health collected from 2008 to 2013, they looked at 44,678 illicit opioid users. Those who'd also used psychedelics had a twenty-seven percent reduced risk of opioid dependence in the past year and a forty percent reduced risk of opioid abuse in the same time frame. Most other drugs showed just the opposite: an association with increased risk. (Interestingly, only marijuana had better numbers, with a fifty five percent reduced risk.)

According to an August 2013 *Popular Science* article, two neuroscientists from the Norwegian

University of Science and Technology found that psychedelics were mostly beneficial to fostering good mental health. They looked at associations between lifetime psychedelic use and mental health with data from the National Survey on Drug Use and Health in the United States. More than thirteen percent of the 130,152 randomly selected survey respondents reported they had used psychedelics like LSD, psilocybin, mescaline and peyote at least once in their life. The study found that psychedelic use was not significantly associated with serious psychological distress, receiving or needing mental health treatment or psychiatric symptoms. "Everything has some potential for negative effects, but psychedelic use is overall considered to pose a very low risk to the individual and to society," clinical psychologist and co-author of the study Pål-Ørjan Johansen said in a press statement. "Psychedelics can elicit temporary feelings of anxiety and confusion, but accidents leading to serious injury are extremely rare."

There has recently been a renewed interest in using psychedelic substances as treatment for psychiatric disorders. Large trials with drugs like ketamine or psilocybin to treat depression, or MDMA to treat PTSD have been conducted, with promising results. In a trial of psilocybin-assisted therapy for treatment-resistant depression for instance, sixty-seven percent of patients were depression-free a week after their two sessions, and forty-two percent remained so after three months.

In May 2018, publications as conservative as *TIME* and *The Weekly Standard* published reviews of Michael Pollan's book, *How to Change Your Mind: What the New Science of Psychedelics Teaches Us About Consciousness, Dying, Addiction, Depression, and Transcendence.* The *BBC* likewise published articles titled 'Magic Mushrooms Promising in Depression," "Magic Mushrooms Can 'Reset' Depressed Brain," and "Could Psychedelics Transform Mental Health?" While the *BBC* tended to focus on research studies in the UK, *TIME* and *The Weekly Standard* focused on Pollan's new book, which was a sweeping and cogent analysis of scientific research in the realm of psychedelia. Pollan concluded that psychedelics presented industrialized medicine with a brave new world in mental health treatment options. "It is all too easy to dismiss what unfolds in our minds during a psychedelic experience as simply a 'drug experience,' and that is precisely what our culture encourages us to do," Pollan writes. "The biggest misconception people have about psychedelics is that these are drugs that make you crazy. We now have evidence that that does happen sometimes — but in many more cases, these are drugs that can make you sane."

In a chapter headed "The Trip Treatment," Pollan observes some university-funded programs as he delves into psychedelic therapies for quitting smoking. The results are significant. As Pollan points out, giving up cigarettes is considered by some to be tougher than getting off heroin. Yet, after being administered a psychedelic, one patient finds that cigarettes simply "became irrelevant," so he stopped smoking. This patient participated in the Johns Hopkins smoking cessation pilot study that combined cognitive behavioral therapy with a compound containing psilocybin. The reason this treatment is effective remains the subject of some debate. Pollan notes, "it may be that the loss of self leads to a gain in meaning," and says explaining the change can't be explained biologically "yet." Pollan compares the patient's experience to the experience of astronauts who report that, having gone into space and looked down at the "pale blue dot" that is their home planet, their ego vanished.

The idea is that taking psilocybin allows patients to confront "the immensity of the universe," thus "making possible a shift in worldview and priorities that allowed them to let go of old habits." Psychedelics can, in short, switch things in the brain around, in what amounts to a reorganization of the mental furniture. Pollan theorizes that psychedelics "relax the brain's inhibition on visualizing our thoughts, thereby rendering them more authoritative, memorable, and sticky."

These effects may also be therapeutic at the end of life. While some of the people Pollan talks with are trying to live longer and be healthier, some have decided to undergo testing with psychedelics as they confront their own impending mortality. "I am the luckiest man on earth," notes Patrick, a man dying of cancer, who participated in an NYU psilocybin trial. Throughout his sessions, he talks of "something beyond this physical body," and the cancer as a "type of illusion." For every report of a "bad trip," Pollan explains, there are a dozen stories of profound enlightenment and happiness experienced by people who have dropped acid or taken mushrooms. Knowing that such sublime beauty is to be found within one's own psyche seems to makes it difficult to retain a self-concept of worthlessness — yet another reason why an experience of mystical consciousness may prove helpful to one recovering from depression or an addiction.

Though substances like psilocybin cannot be expected to "cure addiction" or other human ills simply by swallowing a prescribed pill, if administered with sensitivity to set and setting, they may occasion states of consciousness that could well provide a fulcrum for changes in self-concept, perception of others and the world, and motivation that could constitute a significant contribution to successful treatment. Further, beyond potential applications in medical treatment, these states of consciousness may provide experiential insights into neuroscience and enable us to better comprehend the mysteries of our own being, and humanity writ large.

Chapter Four

"Psilocybin and Societal Well-Being"

In addition to being beneficial to individuals' health and well-being, psilocybin also appears to have societal benefits. In short, psilocybin appears to be good for humanity. In January 2018 *Newsweek*, for example, published an article about a new experimental research program that provided the first evidence that psilocybin might decrease authoritarian views. Scientists from the Psychedelic Research Group at Imperial College London conducted a study using seven participants with treatment-resistant depression, which refers to chronic depression that does not respond to therapy or medication, or most likely a combination of the two. The researchers asked the participants about their relationship with nature and had them respond to questions designed to determine their position on the libertarian-authoritarian axis—in other words, where their personal belief system falls between the opposite extremes of maximizing individual freedoms and restricting them. They then dispensed two oral doses of psilocybin; the first one was ten milligrams and the second was twenty-five milligrams. (A typical recreational dose is usually somewhere between half a gram and five grams.) The participants' responses were assessed after one week, and then again after seven to twelve months had passed, according to psychology news site *PsyPost*. The researchers compared the data to that gathered from seven psychologically healthy control patients who had been asked the same questions, but not given any psilocybin.

The psilocybin group experienced a significant reduction in authoritarian leanings, with noticeable changes holding up even at the seven- to twelve-month mark. The control group exhibited no such change. "These results suggest that psilocybin therapy may persistently decrease authoritarian attitudes post-treatment with psilocybin," the team wrote in a paper describing their research, which was published in the scientific journal *Psychopharmacology*. As the authors wrote in their paper, these findings "tentatively raise the possibility that given in this way, psilocybin may produce sustained changes in outlook and political perspective."

Another study indicates that psilocybin use might diminish violent tendencies in men. In June 2018 *VICE*, for example, reported that a study conducted at the University of British Columbia discovered that men who take psychedelics are half as likely to be violent with a significant other compared to men that do not take psychedelics. The study, which was first published in the *Journal of Psychopharmacology*, adds to a growing body of research that suggests that people who take psychedelics are less violent. Dr. Adele Lafrance, psychologist and one of the co-authors on the study, said, "our research suggests that psychedelic use may actually decrease the risk of violence in the general population, at least in the context of intimate partner relationships. In fact, psychedelic psychotherapy could even be a potential treatment for those at risk for domestic violence." UBC researcher Michelle Thiessen explained that this is the opposite trend you would see for alcohol or cocaine. "Alcohol, cocaine, and methamphetamines, they're all pretty strongly associated with violence," she said. Until recently, "classic" psychedelics like acid, shrooms, mescaline, and ayahuasca were often lumped in with other hallucinogens like PCP, says Theissen, which is part of the reason why scientists have only just begun exploring the drugs' nonviolent associations.

Lafrance's study builds on Thiessen's past work, which looked at domestic violence rates and drug use patterns among male prison inmates. The 2016 study found forty-two percent of men who had never taken psychedelics were arrested again for domestic battery within six years, whereas only twenty-seven percent of men who had taken them were arrested for the same offense. With this latest study, Thiessen and co-authors wanted to expand the sample to include women and the general public. Psychedelic use was associated with less difficulty "regulating" emotions, and significantly less intimate partner violence — but for men only. About five percent of men who had taken psychedelics had met the researchers' definition of domestic abuse, compared to ten percent who had no psychedelic history. "Half is a huge deal," said Thiessen, "that's a lot of people not being hurt." Thiessen says some experimental researchers have looked at fMRI scans of people who are high on psilocybin mushrooms and have seen areas of the brain associated with emotional processing lighting up. Subjects also report an increase in empathy. But other studies have found that the emotional processing extends beyond the "acute" experience of being high, says Thiessen. In other words, a change in worldview may come after you've 'tripped.' This may explain why some people can have a bad trip, but still take some good away from it. "When you're faced with an emotionally charged experience in the future, you're possibly going to reevaluate that differently," says Thiessen.

In study after study, psilocybin seems to awaken the humanitarian within the human. The theme of reconnection, for example, comes up over and over again in these psychedelically-induced mystical experiences and in the research. People struggling with addiction and depression tend to be disconnected from the world and from other people. They fall into these loops of rumination and get stuck, and after a while, reality is blocked out and they're trapped. These drugs seem to lower our defenses and foster a sense of connection with others and with nature. There is still so much to learn about how and why they do this, but it's pretty clear that they do.

Perhaps two of the greatest challenges humans face in the twenty-first century are the way we look at nature and the environmental crisis that has resulted, and tribalism. Both issues are about disconnection. They are both about seeing the other, whether that other is a plant or an animal, or a person of another faith or another gender or race, as objects. Experiencing nature as something that is alive, something that is conscious and part of yourself, makes it very difficult to abuse or degrade. And here we have this natural tool, psilocybin, that allows us to reconnect to the unity of nature.

It is hard to think of a more urgent or promising line of research than mental health, especially when one considers that the least appreciated victim of the Drug War has been people suffering from mental health problems, and this is something that cuts across racial, geographic, economic, and political lines. And we're in this moment in human history in which the culture is changing and calling out for new solutions, and this is something that everyone should be able to get behind. There's a snarling mental health crisis in this country, and it's getting worse. Rates of depression and suicide are climbing, as are addictive behaviors. And it's not just in America; it's a global problem. The world we are living in is putting a lot of pressure on human minds, and some can cope better than others. Depression is the leading cause of disability worldwide. There are three-hundred million cases of depression. That's a lot of suffering, and then add to that the people struggling with anxiety disorder, which is being diagnosed in record numbers. And dealing with addiction, which is probably just a way to deal with the first two problems. If you compare what has happened in mental healthcare to what has happened in nearly any other branch of medicine, you realize how little progress has been made. And now we have got this promising area of psychopharmacology that was abandoned after the 1960s and is now resuming after this crazy generation-long hiatus. It's very exciting, and I think we have the capacity to reduce a lot of suffering in the world.

But how do you prescribe a drug for an entire society? This is the sort of thing that got Timothy Leary, the Harvard psychologist who became the face of the countercultural movement in the '60s, in trouble. He went from treating individuals, which we can do safely, to trying to treat a whole culture, and we don't know how to do that. The tragedy of the '60s was that these drugs, these medicines, got attached to stigmas associated with the countercultural movement. They were used primarily by young people and often they were used carelessly, and we have paid a huge price for these mistakes. It is not that it was all bad, but we allowed these drugs to get unfairly swept away by the reactionary politics of that era. How can we get it right this time? This is one of the issues taken up in part two of this book, which removes psilocybin from sciences' laboratories and returns it to the realm of religion, mysticism, all while considering the law that prohibits the free use of this astounding sacrament and tool.

Chapter Five

"A Short History of
Psychedelic Drugs in Ancient Religion"

For millennia, humans have used a variety of rituals, such as meditation, prayer, fasting, and dance, as well as naturally occurring substances (e.g., plants with psychoactive properties), to increase the likelihood of having a mystical or spiritual experience. For thousands of years, psychedelic drugs played central roles in religious ceremonies as well as having been used for medicinal purposes. Fossil finds dated as old as 10,000 years offer proof of the long history of psychedelics, according to a University of Cambridge report. Much like Native American culture, ancient Asian and European cultures used psychedelics as part of their ritual ceremonies. Psychedelics played such a central role in indigenous cultures that rock paintings of mushrooms from 7,000 BC were portrayed as mushroom deities and labeled as the "Flesh of God." It has been posited that the ancient seers who wrote the *Rig Veda* and extolled the sacredness of soma were experientially familiar with the effects of a mushroom, perhaps amanita muscaria, as were members of early cults that contributed to the formation of Judaism and Christianity. Plato allegedly participated in the Eleusinian Mystery Religion where sacred mushrooms were used as a sacrament. In Ancient Greece the Eleusinian Mysteries required the drinking of a secret potion as part of the initiation ordeal, and Plato made guarded reference to a drug much like LSD in *The Laws*.

Long before industrialized societies became interested in psychedelics, the ceremonial use of plants and fungi containing psychoactive compounds by pre-industrial societies had ascribed them the role of "transporters" to the realm of dreams and to the spirit world. Psychedelics, in short, have long been known for their ability to alter conscious perception, and sometimes produce what seems like transcendent experiences. Throughout the history of psychedelics, these effects have been put to use in religious ceremonies as well as for recreational purposes. The early history of psychedelics centers around the use of naturally occurring substances, such as plants, cacti and mushrooms.

According to Bryn Mawr College, Native American cultures valued the effects of psychedelic drugs as a ritualistic practice carried out during sacred ceremonies. There is also good evidence to suggest that in ancient times the Indian inhabitants of Latin America such as the Aztecs used psychedelic mushrooms. In Mexico's back country ceremonies are still carried out by local priests utilizing an array of magic mushrooms. The Native American Church in the United States makes religious use of peyote in its sacramental ceremonies. This church is a loosely organized association of some 250,000 American Indians representing a number of the principal American tribes.[5] Prehistoric Homo sapiens were so enamored of the fantastic fungi that many formed sacred cults around them in Mesoamerica. Small sculptures of human figures crowned with umbrella-

---

[5] William A. Richards, "The Phenomenology and Potential Religious Import of States of Consciousness Facilitated by Psilocybin," *Archive for the Psychology of Religion*, Vol. 30.

like mushrooms are common throughout the region,

dating between 500 B.C. and 900 A.D.

Chapter Six

"Psilocybin and the Mystical Experience"

In "A Working Paper: Memo on the Religious Implications of the Consciousness-Changing Drugs (LSD, Mescaline, Psilocybin)," Joseph Haven postulated that, "We live in an age of 'the hidden God,' of the silence of the Holy Spirit. Some advocates of 'drug mysticism' suggest that God may himself be at work in these recent discoveries of biochemical science.[6] Mystics had long subscribed to such notions, but there has been a great deal of resistance to such notions in scientific circles. The harsh reality of science is that those who study mysticism and meditation, such as Havens, rarely heard the sound of even one hand clapping among their colleagues in the latter half of the twentieth century. For scientists, creatures of the rational thinking dogmatized by the seventeenth-century Enlightenment, claims of mystical enlightenment have long smacked of self-

---

[6] Joseph Havens, "*Journal for the Scientific Study of Religion*, Vol. 3, No. 2 (Spring, 1964), pp. 216-226.

deception, gullibility, mental disorder, charlatanism, or all of the above. However, a small band of researchers have explored the nature of mystical experiences and other extraordinary psychological happenings to great effect, which has helped this type of recent come to the fore of the mainstream in recent years.

Although mystical experiences cannot be easily diced up and quantified, they affect a surprisingly large number of people. National surveys in the United States and England, for example, find that roughly one-third of adults say that they have had, for example, a moment of sudden religious awakening or felt close to a powerful, spiritual force that seemed to lift them out of themselves. Such experiences may extend far back into human prehistory. According to archaeologists, cave and rock art from Africa to Australia depicts shamans' supernatural encounters, which occurred during conscious states achieved through chanting, dancing, hallucinogenic drugs, or other means.

The most systematic, and arguably novel,

scientific study of how mystical experience alters people's lives took place in 1963; physician Walter Pahnke randomly selected half of a group of twenty Protestant seminarians and gave them the hallucinogenic drug psilocybin before the entire group listened to a radio broadcast of a Good Friday service. Those who did not receive psilocybin got a B-vitamin, thus serving as a placebo. After the service, those who ingested psilocybin reported having had experiences resembling those of classic mystics, such as a feeling of oneness with God or ecstatic visions. The B-vitamin group recalled more mundane reactions. Immediately afterward, participants learned whether they had received psilocybin or placebo. Six months later, the researcher surveyed the participants. After twenty-five years, another researcher contacted seven of those who had received psilocybin and nine who had gotten the placebo. In both follow ups, members of the psilocybin group cited many more positive changes in their attitudes and behavior that they attributed to the Good Friday broadcast than placebo-group members did. Pahnke's experiment seems to indicate that there is indeed some quantifiable spirit or unique personality in each human (and dog and cat for that matter).

Pahnke's study also underscores the falsity of thinking about science and spirituality through an oppositional framework. So much of the research into psilocybin is forcing scientists to deal with spiritual questions, and some spiritual people to deal with scientific questions. More recently, for example, a number of religious leaders have been taking psilocybin to more intimately commune with the supernatural. Rabbi Zalman Schachter-Shalomi, a veteran psychonaut and founder of the Jewish renewal movement, once said: "To understand the depth of religion, one needs to have firsthand experience. It can be done with meditation. It can be done with sensory deprivation. It can be done a number of ways. But I think the psychedelic path is sometimes the easiest way, and it doesn't require the long time that other approaches usually require." Schachter-Shalomi was no stranger to psychedelics. He'd tripped in the 1960s with Timothy Leary and

Ram Dass (Richard Alpert), Harvard psychologists who pioneered research into LSD and psilocybin.

The Johns Hopkins and NYU Religious Leaders study includes what a total of twenty-four Muslim imams, Jewish rabbis, Buddhist roshis, and Hindu, Protestant, and Catholic priests who had never done psychedelics before. In study sessions, they were given capsules of synthesized psilocybin, the active compound in magic mushrooms, and told to lie down with eyeshades on, while wearing headphones that play calm classical or global music. "It's our thought that the foundational underpinnings of the world's religions may stem from a common sense of unity and interconnectedness, and that perhaps there's something very similar about them," says Johns Hopkins psychologist Dr. Roland Griffiths, lead author of the study. "So, what would such an experience mean to someone who's dedicated their life to the study of their own scriptural tradition, teaches spirituality within the context of those traditions, and provides ministry for people in suffering?" It's an exciting question that the researchers hope to, in time, be able to understand better.

A "mystical experience" in clinical terms is defined by feelings of "internal and external unity, transcendence of space and time, ineffability and paradoxicality, sense of sacredness, sense of ultimate reality ('noetic quality'), and deeply felt positive mood." This supposedly matches the descriptions put forth by saints and mystics over millennia. Now, with the dozens of clinical studies demonstrating the efficacy of psychedelic-assisted psychotherapy, mysticism is all too difficult to ignore — especially when the mystical experience is often the mechanism by which patients begin to heal. In the current psilocybin-assisted psychotherapy research, for instance, mystical experiences are helping patients overcome ailments like addiction or end-of-life cancer anxiety. Griffiths and fellow researchers Katherine MacLean and Matthew Johnson showed in a 2011 study that the psilocybin-induced mystical experience could increase personality openness. "In participants who met criteria for having had a complete mystical experience during their psilocybin session, Openness remained significantly higher than baseline more than one year after the session," he wrote.

The professor confirmed the same in a 2015 paper he co-authored. "Although biological mechanisms underlying the mystical experience have not been identified, mystical experiences have a clear operational definition," he wrote. "And the value of mystical experiences in terms of predicting positive outcomes has been empirically demonstrated." These changes can turn a life around. "It seems to predict attributions that people make in the long term to positive changes in their life, perception of self, and compassion for others," Griffith says. For instance, reduced craving scores in cigarette smokers are correlated with the magnitude of the mystical experience: the higher the mystical experience, the fewer cravings. In cancer patients, the higher the mystical experience score, the less anxiety and depression they're likely to report. Even if we don't understand exactly how drug-induced mystical experiences are helping people, it's hard to look past these proven effects. In the coming years, that could force the DEA and FDA to grapple with the concept of legal tripping — and it could change what the modern world thinks about mysticism itself.

"What we're finding is the world itself is not this Cartesian world [with] this duality between the mechanistic, physical, material and the spiritual, ghostly, and abstract," says psychologist Neal Goldsmith, author of *Psychedelic Healing: The Promise of Entheogens for Psychotherapy and Spiritual Development.* "The entire universe is imbued with whatever fundamental stuff, call that God if you want, or subatomic quantum mechanics, but it's this sense that the world is not dualistic, but one whole thing. Then it becomes reasonable that matter would have in it a source or 'magic' essence that initiates healing.[7]

The first really groundbreaking study in the modern era of psychedelic research, was a 2006 study done at Johns Hopkins by a scientist named

---

[7] Madison Margolin, "Psychedelic Drugs Might Actually Tap into a Higher Power," Inverse.com, April 27, 2017.

Roland Griffiths, a very prominent drug-abuse scientist. He found that what the psychedelics did in about eighty percent of cases was induce a mystical experience, which is a spiritual experience that was studied closely by William James at the turn of the twentieth century. A mystical experience has various aspects to it. Prominent among them is a dissolving of a sense of self (ego), followed by a merging with the universe, or with nature, or other people. It's called the noetic quality — this sense that what you're seeing or feeling or learning on this experience has the status of revealed truth. It's not just an opinion — it's objectively true. We have seen this experience all over religious literature since time in memorial: people who have had an experience of communing with the divine. These traits are common, and the fact that you could induce such a spiritual experience with a single administration of a drug is quite remarkable. Many research subjects later reported that these psychedelic-induced mystical experiences were among the top two or three moments in their lives, comparable to the birth of a child or the death of a parent. Now that we can actually induce a spiritual experience using psilocybin, which can be easily made at home, we each can harness access to the mystical experience.[8]

And although it is true that one cannot take psilocybin as a pill to cure one's alienation, neurosis, addiction, or fear of death in the same way one takes aspirin to banish a headache, what psilocybin does do is it provides an opportunity to explore a range of mystical states. It unlocks a door; how far one ventures through the doorway and what awaits one in the realms beyond is largely dependent on non-drug variables, particularly set and setting. What is certain is that both scientists and spiritualists can benefit greatly by focusing on the potentially life-enhancing effects of particular states of consciousness that are experienced from ingesting entheogens such as psilocybin. Given adequate dosage and

---

[8] Bruce Bower, "Into the Mystic," *Science News*, Vol. 159, No. 7 (Feb. 17, 2001), pp. 104-106

interpersonal grounding, the states of consciousness that present themselves often appear to be ingeniously designed by an intrinsic wisdom within the psyche to facilitate healing or unfolding self-actualization.

But how do we even begin to define a term as culturally loaded as "mystical consciousness"? I'm reminded of a well-known verse in the *Tao Te Ching*, which reads, "Those who know do not speak; those who speak do not know." This is the point when it would be wise to cease writing and perhaps play music instead. However, claiming poetic (and noetic) license, I'll do my best to find some words as some of our forebearers have done, notably William James (1902) and Abraham Maslow (1966). They both believed mystical consciousness to be closely associated with Unity, Intuitive Knowledge, Transcendence of Time & Space, Sacredness, and Deeply-Felt Positive Mood. These six categories were also essentially those employed by Pahnke in his classic "Good Friday Experiment" (1963), which in turn were based on the scholarship of Walter Stace

(1960). Hindus express mystical consciousness as the drop of water merging with the ocean. As William James observed, although mystical consciousness may entail profound emotions, it also includes intuitive knowledge — James coined it "the noetic quality" (1902). This aspect could well prove to be the nexus of its therapeutic potential in the treatment of addictions, depression and anxiety.

The form of psychedelic experience referred to in the psychological studies of religion, "mystical consciousness," can best be described as a dimension of experience that, when expressed on paper by an experimental subject and subsequently content analyzed, corresponds to nine interrelated categories. The nine characteristics Stace identified were (1) internal unity (i.e., undifferentiated awareness, unitary consciousness); (2) external unity (i.e., a sense of unity with the surrounding environment); (3) nontemporal and nonspatial quality (i.e., feelings of infinite time and limitless space, transcending usual time and space boundaries); (4) inner subjectivity (i.e., a sense of life or living presence in all things); (5)

objectivity and reality (i.e., noetic quality, a sense that the experience was a source of objective truth); (6) sacredness (i.e., worthy of reverence, divine, or holy); (7) deeply felt peace and joy; (8) paradoxically (i.e., needing to use illogical or contradictory statements to describe the experience); and (9) ineffability (i.e., difficulty of communicating or describing the experience to others).[9]

In summation, "mystical consciousness" is defined as a state of human experience that, when retrospectively expressed, typically can be found to entail expressions of ineffability, unity, intuitive knowledge, transcendence of time and space, sacredness and profoundly positive mood. These mystical and archetypal experiences awaken persons to the reality of the spiritual dimension of life, sometimes expressed as awareness that in everyday

---

[9] Walter N. Pahnke and William A. Richards, "Implications of LSD and Experimental Mysticism," Journal of Religion and Health, Vol. 5, No. 3 (Jul., 1966), pp. 175-208. The Mystical Experience Questionnaire (MEQ) was developed by Pahnke (1963, 1969) as a tool for the evaluation of single mystical experiences occasioned by hallucinogens.

living we actually are spiritual beings who are having physical experiences. As His Holiness, the Dalai Lama, in his respectful dialogues with scientists, reminds us, "The view that all mental processes are necessarily physical processes is a metaphysical assumption, not a scientific fact," and that current neuroscience does not have "any real explanation of consciousness itself." Maslow's concluding words in *The Psychology of Science* likewise evokes the Dalai Lama's sentiment: "Science at its highest level is ultimately the organization of, the systematic pursuit of, and the enjoyment of wonder, awe, and mystery."[10]

Mystical experiences are a common component of religious traditions across human history. Historical descriptions of mystical experience from diverse sources also reveal common themes, suggesting a core experience that cuts across religions and cultures, which is the exact idea behind the NYU

---

[10] William A. Richards, "The Phenomenology and Potential Religious Import of States of Consciousness Facilitated by Psilocybin," *Archive for the Psychology of Religion*, Vol. 30.

psilocybin study in which religious leaders are the subjects.

What is perhaps most amazing about some of the latest research was a study that tested the viability, usefulness, and effectiveness of the Mystical Experience Questionnaire developed by Stace and Pahnke. Mystical experience, in short, could be quantified; science could be religion and vice versa. In addition, surveys showed that approximately thirty to fifty percent of Americans endorse having had a mystical experience or religious awakening. More recently, rigorous double-blind laboratory studies had concluded that psilocybin could reliably occasion mystical-type experiences that were associated with persisting increases in personal well-being, life satisfaction, and positive behavior change. These findings demonstrate an experimental model for occasioning mystical experiences in the laboratory that permits a study of their causes and consequences, an approach that is supported by some philosophers of religion, such as Huston Smith, who suggested that the sacramental use of hallucinogens should be a legitimate object of scientific investigation.

Alan Watts, a renowned theologian, hailed sacramental psychedelic use because it helped those who took them gain a greater "polar awareness." He described polar awareness as an understanding of yin/yang in which a person could more tangibly grasp the notion that things which are explicitly different are implicitly one: self and other, subject and object, left and right, male and female, solid and space, figure and background, pulse and interval, saints and sinners, and police and criminals, ingroups and outgroups. As this awareness became increasingly intense, Watts asserted, a person could more easily feel that they were polarized with the external universe in such a way that they implied the other. "Your push is its pull," he wrote, "and its push is your pull, as when you move the steering wheel of a car."[11]

Both renowned psychologist Walter Houston

---

[11] Alan Watts, "Psychedelics and Religious Experience," *California Law Review*, Vol. 56, No. 1 (Jan., 1968), pp. 74-85.

Clark and Watts perceived mysticism as neither superstition nor vague emotion but, at least in its essential characteristics, an identifiable state of mind, probably the most intense and captivating of which human nature was capable. Clark's "Religious Aspects of Psychedelic Drugs," reminded readers that in the seventh book of *The Republic Plato,* Socrates describes the mystical experience as "the brightest self."

The Mystical Experience Questionnaire

Instructions: Looking back on the entirety of your psilocybin session, please rate the degree to which at any time during that session you experienced the following phenomena. Answer each question according to your feelings, thoughts, and experiences at the time of the psilocybin session. In making each of your ratings, use the following scale:

0 – none; not at all; 1 – so slight cannot decide; 2 – slight; 3– moderate; 4 – strong (equivalent in degree

to any other strong experience); 5– extreme (more than any other time in my life and stronger than 4)

Factor 1: Mystical

1. Freedom from the limitations of your personal self and feeling a unity or bond with what was felt to be greater than your personal self.
2. Experience of pure being and pure awareness (beyond the world of sense impressions).
3. Experience of oneness in relation to an "inner world" within.
4. Experience of the fusion of your personal self into a larger whole.
5. Experience of unity with ultimate reality.
6. Feeling that you experienced eternity or infinity.
7. Experience of oneness or unity with objects and/or persons perceived in your surroundings.
8. Experience of the insight that "all is One".
9. Awareness of the life or living presence in all things.
10. Gain of insightful knowledge experienced at an intuitive level.

11. Certainty of encounter with ultimate reality (in the sense of being able to "know" and "see" what is really real at some point during your experience.

12. You are convinced now, as you look back on your experience, that in it you encountered ultimate reality (i.e., that you "knew" and "saw" what was really real).

13. Sense of being at a spiritual height.

14. Sense of reverence.

15. Feeling that you experienced something profoundly sacred and holy.

Factor 2: Positive Mood

1. Experience of amazement.
2. Feelings of tenderness and gentleness.
3. Feelings of peace and tranquility.
4. Experience of ecstasy.
5. Sense of awe or awesomeness.
6. Feelings of joy.

Factor 3: Transcendence of Time and Space

1. Loss of your usual sense of time.

2. Loss of your usual sense of space.

3. Loss of usual awareness of where you were.

4. Sense of being "outside of" time, beyond past and future.

5. Being in a realm with no space boundaries.

6. Experience of timelessness.

Factor 4: Ineffability

1. Sense that the experience cannot be described adequately in words.

2. Feeling that you could not do justice to your experience by describing it in words.

3. Feeling that it would be difficult to communicate your own experience to others who have not had similar experiences.

Chapter Seven

"Psilocybin and the Law"

Psilocybin mushrooms are regulated or prohibited in many countries, often carrying severe legal penalties (for example, the United States Psychotropic Substances Act, the United Kingdom Misuse of Entheogens Act of 1971 and Entheogens Act of 2005, and in Canada the Controlled Entheogens and Substances Act). On November 29, 2008, the Netherlands announced it would ban the cultivation and use of most psilocybin-containing fungi beginning December 1, 2008. Psilocybin and psilocin are listed as Schedule I entheogens under the United Nations 1971 Convention on Psychotropic Substances. Schedule I entheogens are deemed to have a high potential for abuse and are not recognized for medical use, which is especially odd considering how beneficial they have been demonstrated to be in study after study.

So, what are the historical origins of this criminalization and prohibition of entheogens such as psilocybin? European and American culture has, historically, a particular fascination with the value and virtue of man as an individual, self-determining, responsible ego, controlling himself and his world by the power of conscious effort and will. Nothing, then, could be more lunatic to this cultural tradition than the notion of spiritual or psychological growth through the use of entheogens. A "entheogenged" person is by definition dimmed in consciousness, fogged in judgment, and deprived of will. But not all psychotropic (consciousness-changing) chemicals are narcotic and soporific, as are alcohol, opiates, and barbiturates. Psilocybin, for example, differs from alcohol as laughter differs from rage or delight from depression. There is really no analogy between being "high" on psilocybin and "drunk" on whisky.

The obdurate resistance to allowing use of psychedelic entheogens originates in both religious and secular values. Jewish and Christian theologies will not accept the idea that man's inmost self can be identical with the Godhead, even though Christians may insist that this was true in the unique instance of Jesus Christ. Jews and Christians think of God in political and monarchical terms, as the supreme governor of the universe, the ultimate boss. Obviously, it is both socially unacceptable and logically preposterous for a particular individual to claim that she, in person, is the omnipotent and omniscient ruler of the world – and to be accorded suitable recognition and honor. Such an imperial and kingly concept of the ultimate reality, however, is neither necessary nor universal. In the context of Christian or Jewish tradition an individual declares himself to be one with God, he must be dubbed blasphemous (subversive) or insane. Such a mystical experience is a clear threat to traditional religious concepts. The Judeo-Christian tradition has a monarchical image of God, and monarchs, who rule by force, fear nothing more than insubordination. The Church has therefore always been highly suspicious of mystics because they seem to be insubordinate and to claim equality or, worse, identity with God. Nothing could be more alarming to the ecclesiastical hierarchy than a popular outbreak of mysticism, for this might well amount to setting up a democracy in the kingdom of heaven, and such alarm would be shared equally by Catholics, Jews, and fundamentalist Protestants.

The kingly concept of God makes identity of self and God, or self and universe, inconceivable in Western religious terms. The difference between Eastern and Western concepts of man and his universe, however, extends beyond strictly religious concepts. The Euro/American scientist may rationally perceive the idea of organism-environment, but he does not ordinarily feel this to be true. By cultural and social conditioning, he has been hypnotized into experiencing himself as an ego, as an isolated center of consciousness and will inside a bag of skin, confronting an external and alien world. We say, "I came into this world." But we did nothing of the kind. We came out of it in just the same way that fruit comes out of trees. Our galaxy, our cosmos, "peoples" in the same way that an apple tree "apples." Such a vision of the universe clashes with the idea of a monarchical God, with the concept of the separate ego, and even with the secular, atheist-agnostic mentality, which derives its common sense from the mythology of nineteenth-century scientism. According to this view, the universe is a mindless mechanism and man a sort of accidental micro-organism infesting a minute globular rock which revolves about an unimportant star on the outer fringe of one of the minor galaxies. This "putdown" theory of man is extremely common among such quasi-scientists as sociologists, psychologists, and psychiatrists, most of whom are still thinking of the world in terms of Newtonian mechanics, and have never really caught up with the ideas of Curie, Einstein and Bohr. Thus, to the ordinary institutional-type psychiatrist, any patient who gives the least hint of mystical or religious experience is automatically diagnosed as deranged. From the standpoint of the mechanistic religion he is a heretic and is soul-numbing narcotics are an up-to-date form of spiritual lobotomy. And, incidentally, it is just this kind of quasi-scientist who, as consultant to government and law enforcement agencies, dictates official policies on the use of psychedelic chemicals.

The content of the mystical experience is, in short, profoundly inconsistent with both the religious and secular concepts of traditional Western religious thought. Moreover, mystical experiences often result in attitudes which threaten the authority not only of established churches, but also of secular society. Unafraid of death and deficient in worldly ambition, those who have undergone mystical experiences are impervious to threats and promises. Their sense of the relativity of good and evil arouses the suspicion that they lack both conscience and respect for law. Use of psychedelics in the United States by a literate bourgeoisie also means that an important segment of the population is indifferent to society's traditional rewards and sanctions.

The American or Englishman who claims consciousness of oneness with God or the universe thus clashes with her society's concept of religion and the very social structure it undergirds. In per-capitalistic Asian cultures, however, such a man was to be congratulated as having penetrated the true secret of life. He had arrived, by chance or by some such discipline as Yoga- or Zen-meditation, at a state of consciousness in which he experienced directly and vividly what our own scientists know to be true in theory. For the ecologist, the biologist, and the physicist know (but seldom feel) that every organism constitutes a single field of behavior, or process, with its environment. There is no way of separating what any given organism is doing from what its environment is doing, for which reason ecologists speak not of organisms in environments but of organism environments.

Inability to accept the mystic experience is, in short, more than an intellectual handicap. Lack of awareness of the basic unity of organism and environment is a serious and dangerous hallucination. For in a civilization equipped with immense technological power, the sense of alienation between man and nature leads to the use of technology in a hostile spirit – to the "conquest" of nature instead of intelligent cooperation with it. The result is that we erode and destroy our environment, spreading technocratic metropolization instead of civilization.

The undoubted mystical and religious intent of most users of psychedelics requires that their free and responsible use be exempt from legal restraint in any republic which professes to maintain a constitutional separation of Church and State. To the conforms with the tradition of genuine religious involvement, and to the extent that psychedelics induce that experience, users are entitled to some constitutional protection. Also, to the extent that research in the psychology of religion can utilize such entheogens, students of the human mind must be free to use them. The criminalization and subsequent prohibition against access to entheogens such as psilocybin is a draconian restriction of spirtual and intellectual freedom, suggesting that the legal system of the United States is, after all, in tacit alliance with the monarchical (fascist) theory of the universe and will, therefore, prohibit and persecute religious ideas and practices based on an organic and unitary vision of the universe and law. Despite these embedded contractions woven into the fabric of American "justice," let's consider how a mystic might find refuge in the First Amendment to the *United States Constitution*, which specifically provides that "Congress shall make no laws respecting an establishment of religion, or prohibiting the free exercise thereof . . . Originally, the free exercise clause was intended to secure religious autonomy by placing matters of religion beyond the realm of the federal government. Later, the free exercise clause was applied as a limitation on the states as well. Today, the free exercise clause has taken on added significance because it has become the protector of individuals' religious beliefs and practices. The free exercise clause has also taken an active role in prosecutions for the use or possession of psychedelic entheogens. There are several religious groups (and many individuals) who profess a belief in one entheogen or another. Several religious sects believe that a given entheogen is a sacrament in their religion, akin to the eucharist in the Catholic faith. Other religious groups claim that entheogens simply help them to get in touch with their god. Finally, at least one religious group worships the entheogen as actually being a part of its god. No matter what kind of belief is expressed in the entheogen, by asserting such belief those charged with crimes for possession or use of the entheogen have attempted to shield themselves under the free exercise clause. With few exceptions, this defense has proven unsuccessful.

One of the main ways courts dismissed individuals' attempts to protect their rights with the First Amendment was by arguing that defendants lacked the requirements of sincerity and centrality. In psychedelic entheogen cases, the centrality issue has taken on added significance. Courts have been reluctant to find a belief in entheogen use to be central to a religious belief and therefore have rejected free exercise claims.

Another means with which courts have dismissed First Amendment protection of defendants is by arguing that no long history of the religion had been proven. The Native American Church, conversely, had success because was an established church, first incorporated in Oklahoma in 1918.

Peyotism had roots dating back to 1560 A.D., and the Indians who used peyote were responsible in its use. Responsible in this context meant that peyote was used sacramentally in ceremonies, far removed from the general population, and no children were involved.

The "compelling interests of the state" to prosecute the laws of said state have also been used to deny First Amendment protections. The Fifth Circuit Court of Appeals, for example, once ruled that "Congress may prescribe and enforce certain conditions to control conduct which may be contrary to a person's religious beliefs in the interest of the public welfare and protection of society."

In *District of Columbia in United States v. Kuch* a man belonging to a church that subscribed to the "tenet" that psychedelic substances, such as LSD, were the true Host of the church, not entheogens, had very little success finding refuge behind the First Amendment. What the court found to be interesting was the fact that the church's motto was "Victory over Horseshit!"; its symbol was a three-eyed toad; and its official hymns were "Puff, the Magic Dragon" and "Row, Row, Row Your Boat." The court stated that "one gains the inescapable impression that the membership is mocking established institutions, playing with words and totally irreverent in any sense of the term." The court went on to find the aforementioned facts "helpful in declining to rule that the church was a religion within the meaning of the First Amendment."

The case law indicates that the proper analysis to be applied in a freedom of religion cases consists basically of two inquiries: first, whether the government has burdened a religious practice, and second, whether a compelling state interest justifies the burden imposed. The first inquiry to be made by the court can be broken down into three parts, though each of these parts is very much interrelated to the other two. The court must first ask itself whether a "religion" actually exists. The burden to prove whether there is a religion should properly rest on the defendant (as an affirmative defense), and this question should be decided as a matter of law by the court. Since the First Amendment protects the free exercise of "religion," whether a religion actually exists is a proper question for the court to resolve rather than the trier of fact. In addressing this question, the court should keep in mind that a religion need not be of a conventional nature, and it need not profess any sort of belief in a supreme being.

Rather, religion arguably can consist wholly of ethical and moral considerations. The court should avoid delving into the religion itself, since it is not for the court to decide the validity or feasibility of what one believes. The focus of the inquiry should be prevention of the use of religion as a "limitless excuse" for avoiding all prosecution, resolving any and all doubts in favor of finding a religion. Next, the court should simply look to the religion and the statute in question, and then decide whether there is a burden of some sort imposed upon the religion. All that need be answered at this point is whether there is any burden imposed upon the religion, the degree of the burden being unimportant at this stage of the analysis. The determination should be an easy one to make and once again should be decided by the court rather than the trier of fact. All doubts should be resolved in favor of there being a burden imposed upon the religion. The final part of this first inquiry basically encompasses the "sincerity" test. The question is this: Accepting the religion to be bona fide, does the defendant truly believe in what he professes? This is a wholly subjective determination and, being a factual question, should be determined by the trier of fact. The second inquiry of the two-pronged analysis is whether a compelling state interest justifies the burden placed upon the religion. This stage of the analysis is only reached where the first inquiry is answered in favor of the defendant, i.e., there is a burden placed on defendant's religion. It is at this stage of the analysis that the question of "centrality" and degree of burden should come into play. The test applied is a balancing test, weighing the interests of the state against the interests of the defendant. The scales are weighted in favor of the defendant because a religion is involved, and for the state to tilt the scales back in its favor, it must demonstrate a compelling interest on its part to infringe upon the religion.

In a balance of interests, whether defendant's entheogen use is a central or integral part of his religion becomes a relevant consideration. The more central the entheogen is to the religion, the greater the interest that must be demonstrated by the state. In the same fashion, the less central entheogen use is to the religion, the easier it should be for the state to demonstrate an interest that would justify the burden placed upon the religion. However, in any case the interest must prove to be compelling. The only point of fluctuation should be exactly where the compelling state interest overcomes the defendant's interests in his religious practice. This balancing test is to be performed by the court rather than by the trier of fact. The foregoing analysis is basically that laid down by the Supreme Court. It has been broken down into various parts in an effort to make the analysis more systematic and easier to apply.

The main point to be recognized is that the freedom of religion defense deserves careful consideration when raised and requires the strictest level of scrutiny by the courts. The freedom of religion defense has not met with much success. The courts have not been overly receptive to the defense and have applied various methods to avoid it. Some courts have applied the proper constitutional standards and have used sound reasoning in rejecting the defense. Other courts have simply avoided the proper constitutional guidelines developed by the Supreme Court and instead have relied on questionable Supreme Court decisions more than a century old. Finally, there are those courts that have applied the proper analysis, only to fail in the reasoning used to arrive at their final results. Only the Native American Church has been successful with the defense.

Despite the lack of success of invoking freedom of religion, it is an interesting question as to how the most revered substances of the shamanic world came to be so reviled in the "modern" world. These substances right now are, ironically, "legalized" in that they are placed in Schedule I of the Controlled

Substances Act and, as such, are available for legitimate research purposes only. Any substance can be used and/or abused but some more than others. Cocaine is a Schedule II medication (used primarily but rarely as a topical anesthetic) but illicit cocaine abuse doesn't derive from such approved medical indication. Similarly, it may come to be one day, even soon, that these types of entheogens may be legally available by prescription for specific medical indications including for psychotherapy and/or for spiritual purposes outside of protected religious practice. But such "legalization" requires development through the FDA's system of review for public safety and to clarify risks and benefits and that for the specific indications that benefits do reasonably outweigh potential risks. Though entheogens such as psilocybin are, though non-addictive, still widely and erroneously considered to have a high potential for abuse concomitant to being classified as having no accepted medical use in treatment in the United States and are as such classified as schedule I, there does seem to be slow liberalization of views towards the scientific and even recreational use of psychedelics. The United States and several countries in Europe now acknowledge, for example, the religious freedom of members of the Uniao Do Vegetal and Santo Daime – religions that have expanded from the Amazon Basin and now count members around the world that partake of DMT-containing ayahuasca in their prayer services. Native use of Ayahuasca is legal in Brazil, Columbia, and Peru. The Bwiti faith in west Africa (The Gabon and elsewhere) is also legally sanctioned and has an iboga ceremony – the root bark from the shrub Tabernan; the iboga contains a very long-acting hallucinogenic substance ibogaine.

The Santo Daime are particularly interesting because the group was using ayahuasca as a sacrament in ceremonies in the Netherlands when, in the autumn of 1999, authorities intervened and arrested its leaders. It was the first case of religious intolerance by a Dutch government in more than three hundred years. A subsequent legal challenge, based on European Union human rights laws, saw Santo Daime acquitted of all charges. A similar case in

Spain resulted in the Spanish government granting the right to use ayahuasca in that country. A September 4, 2003, court decision in the United States by the Tenth Circuit Court of Appeals, likewise ruled in favor of religious freedom to use ayahuasca (Center for Cognitive Liberty and Ethics, 2003). As such, the federal government is limited in restricting the practice of one's bona fide religious faith: under the Religious Freedom Restoration Act, the Government must employ a "least restrictive means test" as to whether or not religious practices must be regulated or prevented.

More recently, a New Mexico appeals court ruled on June 14, 2005, that growing psilocybin mushrooms for personal consumption could not be considered "manufacturing a controlled substance" under state law (but it still remains illegal under federal law). In December 2018, Oregon's Secretary of State approved a ballot initiative that would make psychedelic mushrooms legal among licensed therapists. In May of 2019, Denver, Colorado, became the first city in America to decriminalize psilocybin mushrooms after an ordinance written by an advocacy group named Decriminalize Denver was admitted to the ballot, and was narrowly voted in with 50.6% of the vote. The initiative did not actually legalize magic mushrooms, but it did prohibit Denver from spending any resources to prosecute people for their use or possession. In June 2019, Oakland became the second U.S. city to decriminalize psilocybin mushrooms. The City Council passed the resolution in a unanimous vote ending the investigation and imposition of criminal penalties for use and possession of natural entheogens.

It is important to note that what is widely considered to be illicit in one century is sometimes not considered criminal later on. Many of the world's great religious figures were once considered criminal, mad or both. Moses, who is but one example, was a fugitive; the early Christians were accused of hatred of the human race; the religious integrity of George Fox sent him to prison many times; and Martin Luther was forced to maintain his integrity in the shadow of martyrdom. Contemporary America has confronted conscientious objectors whose religious convictions impelled them to resist the draft and watched the Amish sell their ancestral lands rather than compromise their religious convictions by sending their children to state approved schools.

Prosecuting religiously motivated individuals who violate archaic entheogen laws ironically forces violators to conduct their defenses before those who, no matter how well intentioned and experienced in the law, are almost always nevertheless unable to appreciate the defendant's religious experiences. This is not to say that all consumers of psychedelic entheogens are responsible citizens. But at least some will bear comparison with other mystics such as Socrates, Meister Eckhart, and Francis of Assisi, in their apprehension of truth, their compassionate concern for mankind, and their willingness to hold to their vision in the face of threats of imprisonment and extreme punishment.

Chapter Eight

"A Guide For Cultivating Psilocybin"

Disclaimer: Growing psilocybin mushrooms for consumption is a potentially illegal activity, and we do not encourage or condone this activity where it is against the law. However, we accept that people will grow psilocybin mushrooms, and believe that offering responsible harm reduction information is imperative to keeping people safe. For that reason, this guide is designed to ensure the safety of those who decide to grow psilocybin mushrooms. It is important to note that in all but three U.S. states it is legal to purchase spores, which contain absolutely no drug contents. That said, manufacturing psilocybin is prohibited by federal law.

INTRODUCTION

BACKGROUND

This guide is based on Robert "Psylocybe Fanaticus" McPherson's eponymous PF Tek—the method that revolutionized growing mushrooms indoors. McPherson's key innovation was to add vermiculite to a grain-based substrate (as opposed to using grain alone), giving the mycelium more space to grow and mimicking natural conditions. Although his method is a little more labor-intensive than others, often for a lower yield, its simplicity, low cost, and reliability makes it ideally suited to beginners. It also makes use of readily available materials and ingredients, many of which you may already have.

SPORE SYRINGES

The one thing you might have trouble getting is a good spore syringe. This will contain your magic mushroom spores and be used to "sow" them into the substrate. Some growers have reported issues of contamination, misidentified strains, and even syringes containing nothing but water. However, as long as you do your research and find a reputable supplier, you shouldn't have any problems.

If in the United States, I highly recommend procuring your spores from www.mushrooms.com

This is a very reputable source for spores.

All other materials can be easily obtained from Amazon.com, etc.

In any case, after you've grown your first batch (or flush) of mushrooms, you can start filling syringes of your own (see part 4).

WHAT VARIETY SHOULD I CHOOSE?

As you learn how to grow mushrooms indoors, you'll want to decide on a species and strain. Most suppliers offer a range to choose from, but the *Psilocybe cubensis* B+ and Golden Teacher mushrooms are among the most popular for beginners. While not as potent as some others, like Penis Envy, they're reportedly more forgiving of sub-optimal and changeable conditions.

WHAT YOU WILL NEED

INGREDIENTS

- Spore syringe, 10-12 cc
- Organic brown rice flour
- Vermiculite, medium/fine
- Drinking water

EQUIPMENT

- 12 Shoulderless half-pint jars with lids (e.g. Ball or Kerr jelly or canning jars)
- Hammer and small nail
- Measuring cup
- Mixing bowl
- Strainer
- Heavy duty tin foil
- Large cooking pot with tight lid, for steaming
- Small towel (or approx. 10 paper towels)
- Micropore tape
- Clear plastic storage box, 50-115L
- Drill with ¼-inch drill bit
- Perlite
- Mist spray bottle

HYGIENE SUPPLIES

- Rubbing alcohol
- Butane/propane torch lighter
- Surface disinfectant
- Air sanitizer

- Sterilized latex gloves (optional)
- Surgical mask (optional)
- Still air or glove box (optional)

INSTRUCTIONS

The basic PF Tek method is pretty straightforward: Prepare your substrate of brown rice flour, vermiculite, and water, and divide it between sterile glass jars. Introduce spores and wait for the mycelium to develop. This is the network of filaments that will underpin your mushroom growth. After 4-5 weeks, transfer your colonized substrates, or "cakes", to a fruiting chamber and wait for your mushrooms to grow.

NOTE: Always ensure good hygiene before starting: spray an air sanitizer, thoroughly disinfect your equipment and surfaces, take a shower, brush your teeth, wear clean clothes, etc. You don't need a lot of space, but your environment should be as sterile as possible. Opportunistic bacteria and molds can proliferate in conditions for cultivating shrooms, so it's crucial to minimize the risk.

STEP 1: PREPARATION

1) Prepare jars:

- With the hammer and nail (which should be wiped with alcohol to disinfect) punch four holes down through each of the lids, evenly spaced around their circumferences.

2) Prepare substrate:

- For 12 jars, mix 8 cups of vermiculite with 3 cups of water
- Then mix in 3 cups of brown rice flour mix

3) Fill jars:

- Being careful not to pack too tightly, fill the jars to within a half-inch of the rims.
- Sterilize this top half-inch with rubbing alcohol
- Top off your jars with a layer of dry vermiculite to insulate the substrate from contaminants.

4) Steam sterilize:

- Tightly screw on the lids and cover the jars with tin foil. Secure the edges of the foil around the sides of the jars to prevent water and condensation getting through the holes.
- Place the small towel (or paper towels) into the large cooking pot and arrange the jars on top, ensuring they don't touch the base.
- Add tap water to a level halfway up the sides of the jars and bring to a slow boil, ensuring the jars remain upright.
- Place the tight-fitting lid on the pot and leave to steam for 75-90 minutes. If the pot runs dry, replenish with hot tap water.

NOTE: Some growers prefer to use a pressure cooker set for 60 minutes at 15 PSI.

5) Allow to cool:

- After steaming, leave the foil-covered jars in the pot for several hours or overnight. They need to be at room temperature before the next step.

STEP 2: INOCULATION

1) Sanitize and prepare syringe:

- Use a lighter to heat the length of your syringe's needle until it glows red hot. Allow it to cool and wipe it with alcohol, taking care not to touch it with your hands.
- Pull back the plunger a little and shake the syringe to evenly distribute the magic mushroom spores.

  NOTE: If your spore syringe and needle require assembly before use, be extremely careful to avoid contamination in the process. Sterilized latex gloves and a surgical mask can help, but the surest way is to assemble the syringe inside a disinfected still air or glove box.

2) Inject spores:

- Remove the foil from the first of your jars and insert the syringe as far as it will go through one of the holes.
- With the needle touching the side of the jar, inject approximately ¼ cc of the spore solution (or slightly less if using a 10 cc syringe across 12 jars).

- Repeat for the other three holes, wiping the needle with alcohol between each.
- Cover the holes with micropore tape and set the jar aside, leaving the foil off.
- Repeat the inoculation process for the remaining jars, sterilizing your needle with the lighter and then alcohol between each.

STEP 3: COLONIZATION

1) Wait for the mycelium:

- Place your inoculated jars somewhere clean and out of the way. Avoid direct sunlight and temperatures outside 70-80 °F (room temperature).
- White, fluffy-looking mycelium should start to appear between seven and 14 days, spreading outward from the inoculation sites.

NOTE: Watch out for any signs of contamination, including strange colors and smells, and dispose of any suspect jars immediately. Do this outside in a secure bag without unscrewing the lids. If you're unsure about whether a jar is contaminated, always err on the side of caution — even if the substrate is otherwise healthily colonized — as some contaminants are deadly for humans.

2) Consolidate:

- After three to four weeks, if all goes well, you should have at least six successfully colonized jars. Leave for another seven days to allow the mycelium to strengthen its hold on the substrate.

STEP 4: PREPARING THE GROW CHAMBER

1) Make a shot gun fruiting chamber:

- Take your plastic storage container and drill ¼-inch holes roughly two inches apart all over the sides, base, and lid. To avoid cracking, drill your holes from the inside out into a block of wood.
- Set the box over four stable objects, arranged at the corners to allow air to flow underneath. You may also want to cover the surface under the box to protect it from moisture leakage.

NOTE: The shot gun fruiting chamber is far from the best design, but it's quick and easy to build and does the job well for beginners. Later, you may want to try out alternatives.

2) Add perlite:

- Place your perlite into a strainer and run it under the cold tap to soak.
- Allow it to drain until there are no drips left, then spread it over the base of your grow chamber.
- Repeat for a layer of perlite roughly 4-5 inches deep.

STEP 5: FRUITING

1) "Birth" the colonized substrates (or "cakes"):

- Open your jars and remove the dry vermiculite layer from each, taking care not to damage your substrates, or "cakes", in the process.
- Upend each jar and tap down onto a disinfected surface to release the cakes intact.

2) Dunk the cakes:

- Rinse the cakes one at a time under a cold tap to remove any loose vermiculite, again taking care not to damage them.
- Fill your cooking pot, or another large container, with tepid water and place your cakes inside. Submerge them just beneath the surface with another pot or similar heavy item.
- Leave the pot at room temperature for up to 24 hours for the cakes to rehydrate.

3) Roll the cakes:

- Remove the cakes from the water and place them on a disinfected surface.
- Fill your mixing bowl with dry vermiculite.
- Roll your cakes one by one to fully coat them in vermiculite. This will help to keep in the moisture.

4) Transfer to grow chamber:

- Cut a tin foil square for each of your cakes, large enough for them to sit on without touching the perlite.
- Space these evenly inside the grow chamber.

- Place your cakes on top and gently mist the chamber with the spray bottle.
- Fan with the lid before closing.

5) Optimize and monitor conditions:

- Mist the chamber around four times a day to keep the humidity up, taking care not to soak your cakes with water.
- Fan with the lid up to six times a day, especially after misting, to increase airflow.

NOTE: Some growers use fluorescent lighting set on a 12-hour cycle, but indirect or ambient lighting during the day is fine. Mycelium only needs a little light to determine where the open air is and where to put forth mushrooms.

STEP 6: HARVESTING

1) Watch for fruits:

- Your mushrooms, or fruits, will appear as tiny white bumps before sprouting into "pins." After 5-12 days, they'll be ready to harvest.

2) Pick your fruits:

- When ready, cut your mushrooms close to the cake to remove. Don't wait for them to reach the end of their growth, as they'll begin to lose potency as they mature.

  NOTE: The best time to harvest mushrooms is right before the veil breaks. At this stage, they'll have light, conical-shaped caps and covered gills.

WHAT NEXT?

STORAGE

Psilocybin mushrooms tend to go bad within a few weeks in the fridge. So if you plan to use them for microdosing or you just want to save them for later, you'll need to think about storage. The most effective method for long-term storage is drying. This should keep them potent for two to three years as long as they're kept in a cool, dark, dry place. If they're stored in the freezer, they'll pretty much last indefinitely.

The lo-fi way to dry your mushrooms is to leave them out on a sheet of paper for a few days, perhaps in front of a fan. The problem with this method is they won't get "cracker dry." That is, they won't snap when you try to bend them, which means they'll still retain some moisture. They may also significantly diminish in potency, depending on how long you leave them out. Using a dehydrator is by far the most efficient method, but those can be expensive. A good alternative is to use a desiccant as follows:

- Air dry your mushrooms for 48 hours, ideally with a fan.
- Place a layer of desiccant into the base of an airtight container. Readily available desiccants include silica gel kitty litter and anhydrous calcium chloride, which you can purchase from hardware stores.
- Place a wire rack or similar set-up over the desiccant to keep your mushrooms from touching it.
- Arrange your mushrooms on the rack, ensuring they're not too close together, and seal the container.
- Wait for a few days, then test to see if they're cracker dry.

- Transfer to storage bags (e.g. ZipLoc, vacuum sealed) and place in the freezer.

REUSING THE SUBSTRATE

After your first flush, the same cakes can be re-used up to three times. Simply dry them out for a few days and repeat Step 5.2 (dunking). But don't roll them in the vermiculite; just place them back in the grow chamber and mist and fan as before. When you start to see contaminants (usually around the third re-use), drench the cakes with the mister spray and dispose of them outside in a secure bag.

CAPPING

I suggest grinding desiccated mushrooms into powder and then encapsulating the powder in "00" capsules to make ingesting the fruits easier and to get a more consistent dose.

MAKING SPORE SYRINGES

Filling your own psilocybin spore syringes is about as self-sufficient as it gets.

First, you'll need to take a spore print from a mature mushroom, i.e. one that's been allowed to grow until its cap has opened out and the edges are upturned. You should also notice an accumulation of dark purple deposits around the base. These are the magic mushroom spores.

To collect them, remove the cap with a flame-sterilized scalpel and place it gills down on a sterile paper sheet. Cover with a disinfected glass or jar to protect it from the air and leave for 24 hours. Keep the resulting spore print out of light in an airtight plastic bag.

To load a spore syringe, scrape some of the spore print into a sterile glass of distilled water. You can find this at auto supply stores. Then fill your syringe (which should also be sterile) and empty it back into the glass several times to evenly distribute the spores. Fill it a final time and place it inside an airtight plastic bag. Leave at room temperature for a few days to allow the spores to hydrate. You can then keep the syringe in the fridge until you're ready to use it. It should last at least two months.

Psilocybin Cubenesis Dosage Guidelines

Dosage of mushrooms containing psilocybin depends on the potency of the mushroom (the total psilocybin and psilocin content of the mushrooms), which varies significantly both between species and within the same species, but is typically around 0.5–2.0% of the dried weight of the mushroom. A typical low dose of the common species Psilocybe cubensis is about 1.0 to 2.5 g, while about 2.5 to 5.0 g dried mushroom material is considered a strong dose. Above 5g is often considered a heavy dose with 5.0 grams of dried mushroom often being referred to as a "heroic dose." The concentration of active psilocybin mushroom compounds varies not only from species to species, but also from mushroom to mushroom inside a given species, subspecies or variety. The same holds true even for different parts of the same mushroom. In the species Psilocybe samuiensis, the dried cap of the mushroom contains the most psilocybin at about 0.23%–0.90%. The mycelium contains about 0.24%–0.32%.

A study at Johns Hopkins University found that a dose of 20 to 30mg psilocybin per 70kg occasioning mystical-type experiences brought lasting positive changes to traits including altruism, gratitude, forgiveness and feeling close to others when it was combined with meditation and an extensive spiritual practice support program.

Below is the recommended dosage guideline for consuming completely desiccated psilocybin cubenesis (pc) mushrooms based on a grown man weighing between 150 – 200 lbs. Please note, each strain of psilocybin cubenesis mushroom has different levels of the psychotropic alkaloid content known as psilocybin cubenesis and can vary from strain to strain and even from mushroom to mushroom. The guideline below is scientific and based on rigorous research and empirical evidence, but it is still very much an approximation. As such psychonauts should always proceed with utmost caution in experimentation of new strains.

Microdosing

Dose: .5 grams (three - four capsules) of dry cb fruits every third morning (i.e. Monday, Thursday, Sunday, Wednesday, Saturday)

This is a small (micro) dose and not enough for a "trip" in the traditional sense. The microdose of pc releases a small amount of serotonin to the brain, but does not flood the neuro-receptors to the degree a full dose (level one – five) would. Microdosing over an extended period of time can, however, inspire profound spiritual, intellectual, and emotional development and well-being. Studies have proven that microdosing can stabilize and improve a person's mood, productivity, creativity, enhance focus, and provide relief from chronic depression, anxiety, cluster headaches, substance abuse, obesity, and a variety of other chronic maladies. Please note, microdosing will not get one high and is meant to be sacramental. As such, it is not to be simply popped like a pill or drunk like a beer. It is, in other words, imperative that the explorer remind herself why she is microdosing each time she ingests the medicine. If the explorer commits to the regimen, revolutionary changes are likely to occur in that person's life within a year.

Level One

Dose: 1 gram (seven capsules) dry cb fruits

This dose produces a mild "stoning effect" with some visual enhancement such as brighter colors and phantom motions of inanimate objects. Some short-term memory anomalies are also possible, as is confusion in right/left brain communication, causing certain types of music to seem wider and/or more expansive in tonal soundscape than normally experienced.

Level Two

Dose: 2 grams (fourteen capsules) dry cb fruits

Expect bright colors and enhanced visuals such as inanimate objects appearing to pulsate or breathe.

Some two-dimensional patterns become apparent when closing eyes. The user might also experience confused thoughts. Change in short-term memory may also lead to continual distractive thought patterns. A vast increase in introspective and/or analytical and creative thinking also becomes noticeable as the normal brain filter is temporarily bypassed as serotonin floods the neuro-receptors in the explorer's brain.

Level Three

Dose: 3 grams (twenty-one capsules) of dry pc fruits

The user should expect prominent visuals, especially things appearing curved and/or warped patters of kaleidoscopes can often appear on walls, faces, etc. Some other mild hallucinations such as rivers flowing in wood grains or "mother of pearl." Closed-eye hallucinations will also likely appear to be three-dimensional. Also expect some confusion of the senses such as seeing sounds as colors and vice versa.

Time distortions such as "moments of eternity" are also common.

Level Four

Dose: 4 grams (twenty-eight capsules) of dry pc fruits

The user should expect strong and often euphoric hallucinations such as objects seeming to morph into other objects. Also expect a disintegration or splitting of the ego. Inanimate objects may also seem to communicate with the user. The user might also confuse senses, such as mistake hot with cold, soft for rigid, et cetera. Time and even one's sense of reality may also seem to temporarily lose meaning as previously conceived. Out of body experiences can also occur, as is the blending of senses such as being able to see smells, etc.

Level Five

Dose: 5 grams (thirty-five capsules) of dry pc fruits

This is considered a "heroic dose" and it is highly advised that the explorer should go on this adventure only under the supervision of a guide who is not also exploring inner space beyond level-1. Think of this guide as mission control and one embarking on a level-five adventure as an exploratory mission to an unchartered galaxy far far away. The level-five psychonaut should temporarily expect a total separation from reality as it was previously conceived, including a complete collapse of the ego and deconstruction of one's notion that she was a separate entity from time, space, and matter (including other people, animals, trees, the ocean, etc.). The user will, in short, merge with all space and matter in the universe that she can possibly conceive. Level-five, in truth, is nearly impossible to really define or prepare the explorer for. As such, proceed with all caution. However, always remember that nobody has ever died from eating too many shrooms and that the narcotic effect lasts only as long as the enzymes remain in a human's circulatory system, which is rarely longer than twelve hours. And, unlike the euphoria followed by crippling sadness and depression that follows a trip on MDMA and even some batches of LSD, there is no residual negative effects of a pc trip. The only rule when ingesting pc is to just relax and enjoy the adventure.

Epilogue

Aldous Huxley, wrote in *The Doors of Perception* that "most men and women lead lives at the worst so painful, at the best so monotonous, poor, and limited that the urge to escape, the longing to transcend themselves if only for a few moments, is and always has been one of the principal appetites of the soul." Theologian Paul Tillich once remarked during an address to the Hillel Society at Harvard that "the question our century (the twentieth) puts before us [is]: Is it possible to regain the lost dimension, the encounter with the Holy, the dimension which cuts through the world of subjectivity and objectivity and goes down to that which is not world but is the mystery of the Ground of Being?" I believe that in the twenty-first century is as possible as it ever was to commune with the Holy. I believe that psilocybin, coupled with proper set and setting, can be a pathway to the divine and ineffable awe.

This short book, perhaps guide is a better description, has underscored the personal and societal benefits that, research fully indicates, can be harnessed by using entheogens such as psilocybin sacramentally. Using psilocybin has been proven to, under the right conditions, elicit mystical experiences amongst individuals, which can have profound outcomes in revolutionizing the lives of individuals and, by implication, entire societies. But there is also a long history of criminalization of psilocybin and other psychedelics. But the fact that psilocybin has recently been decriminalized at the local level in places like Denver and Oakland speak to the fact that there is a slow though steady liberalization taking place.

www.ingramcontent.com/pod-product-compliance
Lightning Source LLC
Chambersburg PA
CBHW070812050426
42452CB00011B/2007